Live Album

KESTREL POETS

MICK GOWAR

Live Album

POEMS FOR TEENAGERS

VIKING KESTREL

VIKING KESTREL

Published by the Penguin Group
27 Wrights Lane, London W8 5TZ, England
Viking Penguin Inc., 40 West 23rd Street, New York, New York 10010, USA
Penguin Books Australia Ltd, Ringwood, Victoria, Australia
Penguin Books Canada Ltd, 2801 John Street, Markham, Ontario, Canada L3R 1B4
Penguin Books (NZ) Ltd, 182–190 Wairau Road, Auckland 10, New Zealand

Penguin Books Ltd, Registered Offices: Harmondsworth, Middlesex, England

First published 1990
10 9 8 7 6 5 4 3 2 1

The author and publisher gratefully acknowledge the use of the following copyright material in the poem 'For John Lennon'. 'Don't Let Me Down' copyright © 1969 Northern Songs Ltd. 'I am the Walrus' copyright © 1967 Northern Songs Ltd. 'Revolution 9' copyright © 1968 Northern Songs Ltd. Reproduced by permission of EMI Music Publishing Ltd and International Music Publications.

Filmset in Monophoto Ehrhardt
Printed in Great Britain by
R. Clay & Co. Ltd, Bungay, Suffolk

A CIP catalogue record for this book is available from the British Library

ISBN 0-670-82483-6

To Eleanor and Ned Trathan

Contents

Memories of Northern Ireland

I

The car slows to a stop. I look out:

A square block squats
Encased in steel shutters,
Entombed in six-inch bomb-proof armour plate.

Another Army Post. I look away.
Only my second day in Northern Ireland
And I'm getting quite blasé already.

Then suddenly
from out of nowhere
a tall man wearing jeans and sneakers
dashes to the car
pulls open my unlocked door
and grabs my hand: 'Mick Gowar . . .?'

My heart stops. 'Welcome to our library!'

II

The day the undergraduate was shot
In Queen's, Belfast (a Tit-for-Tat),
Liam's kids came rushing home from school
With skull masks bought for Hallowe'en.

'I'm sorry, but you'll have to wear them
In the house –' 'Oh – *Daad!*'
'I'm sorry, kids, no Trick-or-Treats this year . . .'

Returning from the pub just after twelve
Caroline puts on a Death's Head mask,
Pulls down her sweater, bares a shoulder,
Drapes one leg across a kitchen stool

And sings 'Lily Marlene' in broken-Dietrich.
Then, to drunk applause,
'Falling in Love Again'.

III

At dinner Liam says: 'You've two days left,
So is there anything you'd like to see?'
I struggle to recall a half-lost fact –
'That lake . . . the famous one, you know?' 'Lough Neigh?

You wouldn't rather see the tourist spots?
The Most-Bombed-Bar-In-Europe – how's that sound?
That's what the British mostly want to see:
The Divvis, Lower Falls, Andersonstown.

Think of the disappointment if you balk
The chance to walk the very pavements where
The bloody Shankhill Butchers used to stalk
In favour of a breath of country air.

What will your earnest left-wing friends all say?
– *Faced with reality, he turned away*?'

IV

We stop the car
To gaze across the Foyle
To where the Bogside, Derry used to be:

A tiny patch of corporation Lego
Built to replace the terraced rows
Of houses, shops and pubs. Homes
I'd seen burning nightly on TV.

At our backs a Protestant estate.
And on the end wall of the terrace,
Like a tattoo on a huge communal arm –
A giant, garish horseman facing out
Across the valley, flanked by Union Jacks.
Beneath the prancing hoofs, the legend:
'God Save King Billy! No Surrender!'

V

Beneath his gaze
A gang of kids played Pitch and Toss.
I took a photograph of him to show
The kids back home,
And wondered if they'd know . . .

'King Billy?' Blank.
'Who's he?' I give a clue:
'Billy's short for William –'
'Oh, yeah – *him*.
I know the one you mean:
He had a famous battle by the sea;
He was the one who got an arrow in the eye.

It's all in pictures on a tapestry:
1066 and that – we did it in Class Three.'

Playing Our Song

He was never one for talk, you know –
He hadn't got the knack, he used to say.
'Words are for the clever ones – not me.'

We'd been going out a month or two,
But I was about to pack him in
(The strong and silent bit was getting on my wick.)

Then two days before Valentine's
He gave me this LP,
His first and only gift.

He slouched in (in his usual way),
Muttered: 'I bought this yesterday.
Thought you might like to hear it. OK?'

And left.
He wouldn't stay to lunch.
My parents talked too much, he always said.

I've got it here – the band's Plain Speech,
The album's called, 'The Way It Is'.
I hadn't heard of it before

But on the sleeve,
Beside the title track, I saw
A mark just like a pencil tick.

I put it on: side one, track two –
'*Baby, Baby please don't go.*
Baby, Baby I love you so!'

Then I knew what he was trying to do;
It wasn't just a record –
Every word was true.

I nearly wore that record out,
I memorized each word, each line,
Each note, each pause –

Between the lines, between the tracks –
Till every tiny sound became
A secret sign between us.

When we went out together down the pub,
I used to hum a snatch or two
And watch his face;

Watch for a secret smile,
A squeeze of my hand
Beneath the table . . .

But he was much too shy to show
How much it meant
In front of all his mates.

And then the roof fell in.
He came to see me, looking
Shifty and uncomfortable:

'You know that record?
Have you finished with it? Only
I told Martin he could borrow it next.'

I didn't smash it round his head.
You can't break vinyl
Like you can break a heart –

But I deserved it. What a fool I'd been!
I should have known
He wasn't shy; he wasn't quiet –

He was just plain stupid,
Thick as two short planks . . .
And so was I!

Desert Island Discs

Well Sue, it all began when I was two or three
  And heard 'The Little Cloud That Cried'
Coming from the wireless in the lounge.
  (Johnny Ray – 'Nabob of Sob' – remember?
He cried all the way to the bank.)
  Immediately I know: this is it,
My kind of music. I can cry – I can cry too!
  We wail in unison . . . and I'm hooked for life.

Seven or eight: interrogated by my older cousins
  Brian and Richard, 'Do you know who
Buddy Holly is?' I don't. 'Course I do!'
  'OK then –' smirk, gloat '– tell us what he sings.'
I rack my brains for something that sounds right:
  'How much is that Holly in the window?'
They laugh till Brian is nearly sick.
  That teaches me a lot – a lot.

Next, The Shadows. Three of us – nine, ten years old –
  Miming to 'Apache' with plastic toy guitars and
A bucket drum-kit. No words (less chance of getting
  Something wrong). We get the footsteps right –
That seems the most important thing to do.
  Hey! This Pop Star stuff is easy!
Next day, Geoff's big brother buys a real guitar.
  We find out – instantly – it isn't.

Twelve years old: fingers bruised and bleeding –
   Trying to hold down barre chords on
An impossible, unplayable, ten quid guitar:
   The key to 'Love Me Do', 'I Wanna Be Your Man'
Just out of reach – but only just. After all
   It's only three chords . . . but which three?
I buy Bert Weedon's *Play in a Day* book –
   And find I can't. Give up at 'Bobby Shaftoe'.

At fourteen, fifteen we're all Stones fans. The Beatles
   Are a load of softies! My Mum and Dad
Like The Beatles; they play on *Sunday Night*
   at the London Palladium; even the Queen's Mum
Likes The Beatles. And they've stopped touring.
   It's obvious to us – The Beatles are finished!
Then they release 'Revolver', 'Penny Lane'
   And 'Strawberry Fields Forever',

'Sergeant Pepper'. Then comes Acid Rock –
   Moby Grape, Electric Prunes, The Grateful
Dead . . .
We form a band. All we need is
   A really stupid name, beads, flowery shirts and –
Wait a minute! Rick says we need the Motown Sound
   And sharkskin suits – 'I gotta – gotta – gotta –
Be a Soul Man!' Well? Which will it be?
   We can't do both – we can't afford the clothes.

Just in the nick of time we get the Blues –
  Phew! No more indecision. We follow the Party Line:
Unsmiling seriousness; nothing that isn't a twelve-bar;
  Nothing that isn't copied note-for-note
From B.B., Freddie, Martin Luther King.
  The clothes are cheap, but the right guitars are
Astronomical! We hire them, and the amps, for gigs;
  But the scowls of dedication are our own.

Thank God for Rod and the Lads! We couldn't keep
  A straight Face any longer. Pub Rock – 'Good Time
R & B' – or, to put it another way: pissed.
  'Never a Dull Moment' on stage or off –
Never a gig without a brown ale in one hand,
  A double Bells (no ice, no water) in the other.
'How can you play guitar in that state?'
  'Easy – Bottle-neck! Har! Har! Har!'

Now: all I play is the Stereo. And sneer
  At what my kids like: 'Load of bloody noise!
Listen to this, it's better than that synthesizer crap'–
  McCartney's bass, Keith Richards' rhythm guitar,
Clapton turning the 'Key To Love' or to 'The
Highway'.
  They sneer in turn, as I sneered when my father
Played me Peggy Lee or Woody Herman: 'Listen to this,
  Son. This is real music – real music . . .'

Blue Peter

'I'll just run through the recipe again:

Any nuts without the shells
(Unsalted peanuts only, please remember),
Millet (stripped) and sunflower seeds –
Or any packet wild-bird seed is fine.

Mix thoroughly and weigh.

Add half the weight of melted fat.
Lastly, stir it all together
And put it in the fridge to set.'

A wild-bird cake.
To keep the birds alive in this,
The coldest winter anyone remembers,
Is easy. A child can do it.

Ten minutes later on the *News*:
'Another day of pensioners found
Dead from cold
In London, Glasgow, Manchester . . .'

A million children – maybe more –
Still watching.

How to Make a Fortune and Rule the World

This is the toy that Jack built:

The Ultimate Toy!
A toy that was FREE!
(You think Jack was crazy?
Just wait and see . . .)
No catches, no coupons, no packet tops,
Completely Free
from all the best shops!
(And from all the tatty ones too . . .)

This is the world's most popular toy,
the free toy that Jack built.

Not only was Jack's toy free,
it was all that a toy could be:

The Ideal Gift for boys
and girls –
It had laser-beam eyes
(and shoulder-length curls)
it was covered in muscles
(but cuddly too)

it was armed to the teeth
(and a sweet baby-blue)
it flew through the air
(it had washable hair)
it had
  thousands and thousands of outfits to wear
and that's what made Jack a Billionaire!
There are lots of very expensive things
  to buy for the toy that Jack built.

The toy was free, true enough.
But when you opened the box . . .
'Oh, No!'
Your toy was all in the buff!
Stark naked! That was the hitch,
Jack's toys didn't have a stitch.

(And that was the snare,
because the toy socks alone cost £5 a pair!)

Yes, you pay through the nose
  for the clothing that goes
    with the great toy that Jack built.

But the clothing was only the start.
Jack's TV ads cut to the heart
of every child in the land:

'Hey, Kid!
Look at your toy.
I bet it looks sad.
Why? 'Cos it needs a home
so go ask your dad
to buy you one.
But don't delay!
Your toy needs a home – Today!'

So every boy
who owned a toy,
bullied and nagged
until poor old Dad
had been dragged to the shops to buy him:
The Atomic-Powered-Battle-Station-Star-Cruiser-Moonbase
ADVENTURE DOME!
(£254.99)
With the
Clip-on
Computer-command
Booster-module

Plus
the self-docking
Galactic combat
(Brroom–brroom!)
Moon-bike!
(only £149.99 extra)

And every girl
whose pride and joy
was the cutesie-pie version
of Jack's great toy,
sobbed and moaned until she owned:

The Powder-Pink-Dream-House-And-Beauty-Parlour-Sauna!
Comes complete with
salon-style hair-driers and
curling tongs that
really glow!
(£254.99)

And don't forget
the combined
swimming-pool-and-stable-block.
Comes with
patio-style paved surround
and
(Boing–boing!)
real sprung diving-board!
Plus
a doll-size barbecue for
'outdoor entertaining!'
(only £149.99 extra)

That's the gear that costs a King's Ransom!

And here are Jack's profits – aren't they handsome?
All from the toy that Jack built.

But Jack wasn't finished:
he had a new wheeze.
Every toy would need friends
or enemies,
so that was the next campaign:

'Hey, Kids!
Can you imagine life without chums?
Oooooooh!
Well you know, toys get lonely too,
so go ask your mums
to buy right away
a pal for your toy:
this one for girls,
this one for boys.
Tell her:
"Mum! If you love me as much as you say,
then you'll take me to town
and we'll buy one – Today!"'

That was too much:
Jack's adverts were banned.
But not before every child in the land
had either:

SNUGGLO!
The cuddliest pony in the world
and the best friend
every girl's toy should have!
(Fully washable
because SNUGGLO
is made from
real pony skin!)

Comes complete with
show-jumping fences
and
BURLEY!
The friendly, freckle-faced stable-girl
to do the mucking out.
(only £269.95 plus VAT)

Or:

FIREMASTER!
Firemaster threatens to destroy
the entire universe!
His atomic-reactor breath can
(huurrrgggh!)
melt whole cities in seconds!
Only your toy
can defeat FIREMASTER
in inter-planetary combat . . .

Hey, Sonny?
Would you let the galaxy perish!

Comes complete with
HALITOSI-DEATH-RAY
and batteries
(only £269.95 plus p. & p.).
And from the toys came the books
from the books came the stage-shows,
then the posters, the wallpapers,
lunch-boxes, videos . . .

Jack's success just didn't stop!
Jack even went into Pop:

Here is the single,
a track from the album
of the theme from the film
of the play of the book
which was

Based on the toy that Jack built.

Jack was so famous,
Jack was so wealthy,
Jack was so cunning,
Jack was so stealthy –

What more could he do?
Could he top his success?
Can you guess . . .?

Jack was American
(I forgot to say).
He became so rich, they made him
President Jack of the USA:

And at Jack's slightest whim
every head must bow;
'cos you should see the toys
that Jack's building NOW . . .

The Hawk in the Train

Springtime in Cambridgeshire. An elderly Paytrain
Limps across the grey-green fens
Under a leaden sky. I sit beside the window
Trying not to look outside. 'Brandon –'

The guard growls. 'Next stop, Brandon.'
The carriages totter over the rusty points.
The ancient diesel engine shudders
To a halt. No one gets out.

Then a sudden twitter of excitement:
Two young men, each with a falcon on his wrist,
Have climbed aboard. Two kids rush up
To pet the birds – are stopped,

Warned to approach slowly, quietly.
'Then maybe – if you're very careful . . .'
Helmeted like medieval knights, the hawks
Accept the tentative, one-fingered strokes

As tribute. One lifts a foot in slow salute
Exposing cruel talons. The children shrink back,
Giggling nervously, and are called back to their seats
By parents anxious at the sight of claw and beak.

Freed, the two men take the empty seats
In front of me. They nod a friendly greeting,
Hoping for a chat. Not native fen-men, obviously.
The two blind hawks sit motionless.

I ask them if they've been to some Country Fair
Demonstrating Falconry (out here, you see,
We're very keen on killing birds). No, no! They're
Both appalled at the use of hawks for blood sports.

No. These birds are working birds, on contract
To the US Air Force Tactical Bombing Wing.
The runways, so they tell me, in the spring
Are plagued by flights of nesting birds.

(This is the Pentagon's nightmare:
A bird flies into the intake of a jet
Taking off *and armed*, and in a flash –
No more eastern England . . .)

So these two birds are flown –
Once, twice a week – along the runways.
Airborne deterrence, and it works.
Somewhere behind us, an F1–11

Climbs into the grey sky, heading east.
Hearing the roar, the younger hawk
Jerked from his coma, shrieks:
'A-Wake! A-Wake! A-Wake!'

A Sporting Gun

Frieda lives outside our village,
Frieda has three children
And a dog:

Her husband died two years ago,
She has to manage
On a pension.

Frieda's very sharp,
She's quick and small,
She's clever . . .

(But some say Frieda's sly and crafty,
Always quick to take advantage.)

It's six months now since Frieda
And her children
And her dog moved in.

She's got the garden working hard,
Growing vegetables.
She's clever . . .

(But some say Frieda's sly and crafty,
  Always quick to take advantage.)

Only five foot tall
  With short broad hands
    She'll turn to anything:

Jobs a man not skilled
  Would never try –
    She'll do,

And real hard work –
  Digging like a navvy
    All day long

As if her life
  Depended on it.
    She's clever . . .

(But some say Frieda's sly and crafty,
  Always quick to take advantage.)

One day (a month or so ago, I guess)
  Frieda's digging up some spuds
    When, round the corner

Up the path, heading for the house,
  Waddles a fat, white
    Aylesbury duck –

Cheeky as you please!
Frieda's up and running
Through the house

Grabs her husband's shotgun
And a box of shells –
Loads up on the run . . .

(On the front path, sitting duck
Is standing at his ease . . .)

Frieda stops:
Snaps up the barrel.
Aims – *Kerblam!*

Half an hour later, Frieda's digging
While the dead duck's
Hanging in the shed;

The gun, racked
Like a guilty secret
In the closet.

A fat and well-dressed woman,
Looking very worried
Hurries up the path.

Frieda doesn't know her.
The woman stops;
So does Frieda.

'I live just up the road,' the woman says,
'We've only just moved in.
We're *awfully* worried –

My little daughter Lucy's
Pet white duck
Has wandered off:

She's had it since it had a broken wing.
You can't mistake it
Walks around just like a little dog.

Have you seen a little duck?
She's ever so upset . . .'
But Frieda's clever . . .

(Some say she's sly and crafty,
Always quick to take advantage.)

'*No!*'
Says Frieda,
Quick and bright –

'But if I do
I'll surely let you know.
I hope you find the duck all right!'

Frieda's clever . . . Some say she's
Sly and crafty –
Always quick to take advantage.

(Some might say she's cruel as well,
But I don't know . . .)

Jill

My aunt Jill died when she was
two years old, and was laid to rest
in a coffin no bigger than a doll's house

beneath a doll-sized headstone.
'Dearly loved and sorely missed . . .'
The inscription could no more express

the desolation my grandparents felt
than the bald facts on her death certificate:
'Cause of death: Gastro-enteritis.'

Nothing could be done to save her.
But every year on her birthday
my grandparents, then my parents

placed a simple child's posy
on her grave. Only two years,
but it was still a life

that could be celebrated . . .
until last summer.
My parents made their usual visit

to the cemetery, but couldn't find her.
Stupid. How could they make
such a mistake. Impossible.

Carefully they retraced their steps,
checked all the usual landmarks –
but her grave had vanished.

There was, of course, an explanation.
'Over the past financial year
in order to release tied-up capital . . .'

The cemetery had been sold.
And any grave not bought outright
before a certain date, had been removed.

'But with respect and reverence.'
Returfing and relandscaping had started
as soon as the JCBs had finished.

All trace of her wiped out as if she'd never been:
a second death
more final than the first.

Mourners once feared the 'Resurrection men'
like Burke and Hare;
now we must learn to fear the men in suits.

For John Lennon – Introduction

When John Lennon was murdered in New York, the one question that was asked again and again in the many tributes and obituaries was simply: Why? There seemed no reason why a rock musician, no longer as famous or controversial as he had once been, should be a target for 'assassination'. It seemed clear from all the reports I read at the time that Mark Chapman, John Lennon's killer, was insane: but in what way was he insane? Did he kill John Lennon – as he might have killed anyone who had been walking down the street – for the sheer pleasure of killing? Was he another case of the frustrated nonentity grabbing a moment of fame in the only way he could think of: as the famous killer of a famous man?

I attempted to write a poem at the time as my way of trying to think it through, of trying to work out a few answers to some of the questions that baffled me and a lot of other admirers of John Lennon. I failed. I didn't have enough information.

Over the past nine years, I've read enough books about The Beatles and John Lennon to feel that I have at least some idea of what Mark Chapman *thought* he was doing. But I still can't say I truly understand. His reasons – if you can call them reasons – still seem to me to be mad, but they do seem to have a kind of awful, perverted logic.

He was a fan of John Lennon – more than a fan, he became obsessed by John Lennon. The obsession grew until eventually he came to believe he *was* John Lennon: he called himself John Lennon, he even married a Japanese woman. Then, possibly as a result of reading a magazine story, he seemed to come to the decision that John Lennon was a phoney, and that he – Mark Chapman – was the real John Lennon.

Chapman arrived in New York with a gun, some Beatles cassettes and a novel *The Catcher in the Rye*. On the night of 8 December 1980 – having earlier that day met John Lennon briefly and had his picture taken with him – Chapman shot John Lennon as he was returning home to his apartment in the Dakota building. Despite being rushed to hospital in the back of a police car, John Lennon had already lost too much blood from his wounds to be resuscitated.

John Lennon believed he had a lucky number: 9. He used the number 9 in several of his songs, including 'Revolution 9' on 'The White Album' in which 'number nine . . . number nine . . .' is chanted over a bizarre, whirling cacophony of sound.

But it would seem that John Lennon was wrong; 9 was not his lucky number. If you add the separate figures of the year 1980 until you get a single figure, in the way numerologists do, the answer is 9. And, as several biographers have pointed out, because of the time difference between the USA and Britain the date of his death by British time was not 8 December, it was 9 December.

For John Lennon

(Murdered 8/9–12–80)

I

It was a very mild day,
unusual for December in New York.
A perfect day
for a stroll in Central Park,
or to join the crowds
waiting patiently
in front of the Dakota.

'Mr Lennon –'
'Yes?'
'Would you sign my album?'
'Yeah, sure.
What's yer name, son?'
'John.'
'John what?'
John Lennon.

The sudden explosion
of a flash-bulb.
'Did I have my hat on?
Shit! I didn't want my hat on –'

Two faces slowly surface
on a blurred Polaroid.

Barely noticed,
you walk on
to the waiting limousine.

II

An hour goes by.
Then another. And another . . .
His fingers flick through
the pages of a book,
but in his mind's eye
he reads again the slick,
glossy magazine story

about a forty-year-old
businessman
who watches too much TV,
adores his wife and baby son
and has an estimated fortune
of £250 million –

'*Phoney, phoney, phoney.*'
He searches the pockets
of his blouson jacket
and clutches the cassette.

Only he can hear the voice
of the real John Lennon
inside his head,
urging him on:

'Don't let me down!
Don't let me down!'

III

'I am he as you are he
and you are me and we
are all together . . .'

Half-hidden in shadow
he is waiting –
like a lover,
like *The Catcher in the Rye*
with a .38 –

chanting those words
over and over and over.
He is you;
he has become John Lennon.
You are his false reflection.

Out of many
shall come one –
The car stops. Doors open.
You start to cross the sidewalk

'Mr Lennon . . '

IV

'Do you know who you are?'

A nod.

Blood
Pumps
Over the back seat of the car

Blackness
Closing in
'Number nine –
number nine –
number nine . . .'
Void

Famous Last Words

'I won't be late back. I'm going to Jon's party –
it's only down the road . . .'

Why won't you *listen*?
Just let me explain –
Please? Give me a chance,
It won't happen again.
   Look, it wasn't my fault.
   No, it wasn't my fault:
      It was all 'cos the bus didn't come.

The 99 bus –
Oh, didn't I say?
The bus from the disco
(It was miles away!)
   Well, the bus didn't come,
   And that's why, Mum,
      I didn't get home until quarter to one
         When I said I'd be just down the road.

Jon's party? Oh, that
Was a right load of tat . . .
   Well, actually it was OK,
      But Dave didn't know anybody and so
      He got all shirty and wanted to go.
Then Joe says: 'I know a party – not far.
Let's ring up my Dad and we'll go in his car!'

So we went to this other place,
I don't know where,
But the food was all gone
And the parents were there!
  Then Dave says: 'It's poxy!
  Let's all share a taxi
    And go to this disco I know.'

So we had a good laugh
In the taxi till half
  The way there we were all cracking up
    At this really good joke,
    When the cab-driver bloke –
For no reason at all –
Goes right up the wall
  And says: 'Right! You can get out and walk!'

So we finally get there:
It's 'Jackets and Ties.
Over-21s only.'
We give it a try.
  And we're told to 'get lost!'
  What a cheek!
    So we go to the bus-stop,
    We wait at the bus-stop –
      And the bus doesn't come.

So, that's why, Mum,
I didn't get home until quarter to one
When I said I'd be just down the road.

. . . Oh, no! That's not fair!
You don't understand:
  I couldn't say no.
  I couldn't not go.
    It *wasn't* my fault,
    No, it wasn't my fault –
      It was all 'cos the bus didn't come . . .

A Sense of Balance

£

According to Social Inquiry Reports
Mr X has a chronic drink problem.
In 1980 he received a sentence of
6 months imprisonment for stealing
goods to the value of 14.97

When at liberty he lives
in a flat without curtains
In 1982 he received a sentence of
9 months imprisonment for stealing
goods to the value of 10.71

or carpets, or a cooker
In 1984 he received a sentence of
150 hours Community Service
for stealing 2 joints of meat
and a shirt. Value unknown —

and only a few sticks of
second-hand furniture,
In 1985 he received a sentence of
15 months imprisonment for stealing
2 tins of paint and cash. Total value 16.41

as the DHSS have refused him a grant for essential furnishings.	£
He is currently on remand in HM Prison, following another minor shop-lifting charge.	
Average cost of imprisonment for the year ending 1985 (*per week*)	£ *265.00*

In Detention

or The End of Civilization as We Know It

You're here because there's something I must say:
After last lesson I checked the pencils
– This is serious, pay attention, boys –
I discovered four – yes, four – were missing;
And we know, don't we, it's *not* the first time.
We're going to get this sorted out today.

Stealing. Yes, lads, that's what it is! Pencils
Don't sprout legs and walk – don't snigger, boys!
Until someone owns up, you'll be missing
All your breaks and staying in each lunchtime –
The whole class in detention – every day!
Has anyone got anything to say?

Anyone prepared to tell the truth, boys?
Well? I'm waiting. So, you don't mind missing
Your breaks? Neither do *I*! I've all the time
In the world . . . We can just sit here all day
If need be, till someone is prepared to say –
Come on, boys, what happened to those pencils?

This may seem a fuss for a few missing
Pencils, but *I* know that's how all big-time

Crooks start off: maybe just pencils today;
Tomorrow – armed robbery! Experts say
Most murderers start by stealing pencils!
So think on that – it's frightening, eh, boys?

One boy is to blame, but in the meantime
The whole class must be kept in every day!
You know who you are; have the guts to say:
'I did it.' Admit you took the pencils
And we'll say no more about it. Look, boys,
I'm going to turn my back: if the missing

Pencils are returned, we'll call it a day.
I think you'll agree, no one could say
Fairer than that. As long as the pencils
Are on my desk before I count ten, boys . . .
What did you say, lad? You've found the missing
Pencils? Where? Oh-HO! So, all the time

Those missing pencils had been *hidden*, eh?
Which of you boys did it? Will someone say?
Don't waste my time – we haven't got all day . . .

The Holly Oak

The wind that blew my seed,
The rain that nourished me
Were all you, One Great God.

By your will the desert
Did not swallow me. I grew
Tall and straight and true

To honour you,
God of Fire and Water
Air and Desert.

Then men with axes came
To cut me down.
Was this your will?

And were these men also you
As you are air and fire and desert?
Were their axes you?

And who was he,
Nailed to my crucified body
On that bare hill of rock,

Who in that hour
When your light was lost to me
Cried in my voice:

'Oh God,
My God –
Why have you forsaken me?'

Vespers, 1990

'He's got his eyes closed
hanging there,
but he can see

into everything –
into souls he looks –
and he can heal people

like cripples and children;
and he can make stuff
like bread and fish and that.

In church, the priest says,
'This is the Body and Blood of
Our Lord Jesus Christ . . .'

Does it really turn into
flesh and blood?
Dracula, he drank blood

and only ice or water
or a stake through his heart
or the cross could kill him.

They nailed Jesus to a cross.

But he came back to life
and he can see us all
and everything we do –

Oh, Gentle Jesus, meek and mild
watch over me while I sleep . . .
But please

don't come through my window
in the night,
or anything like that –'

A Simple Faith

I

It's time to pick options. Time to choose
Which subjects to keep on, which ones I'll need

At GCSE. Biology for nursing?
Geography and languages to spread His word?

My teachers say it's up to me;
They're wrong, of course

God has a plan for me.

And Martin, Sam and Janet, Susan, Neville –
Everyone at House Group all agree

The Lord will tell me what he wants from me.

He told Sam and Janet when to get engaged.
They prayed, He spoke,

He told them what to do.

Martin's new job, Neville's flat,
Susan leaving university;

He spoke to each of them,
And He will speak to me –
I have pledged my life to Him.

II

I should have handed in the forms today –

I couldn't. He hasn't spoken to me.
He hasn't told me what He wants.

Martin, Sam and Janet, Susan, Neville say
It's all part of His plan

To test my Faith. A sure sign that
He has a very special job for me!

III

Last night at House Group, we all prayed
For me to have God's guidance.

Martin, Sam and Janet, Susan, Neville all agree
That I must pray and fast –

They say I have to prove my love for Him.
That's what He's waiting for . . .

IV

Two weeks
And still no answer.

What would I do
Without my House Group?

Last night
Martin, Sam and Janet

Stayed with me.
All night

We prayed
For Guidance.

Their Faith is
So much stronger.

They must love God
So much more than me.

If I was more like them,
Would God speak to me . . .?

Seance

We used to talk with spirits of the dead.
   In a clapped-out caravan jacked up on bricks
Down at the bottom of Tim Jones's garden.
   Tim and Rick and Pete and me –

We'd slope off to the caravan, pass five Park Drive
   Around, light up, spread out the Lexicon cards
On the flop-down plywood table-flap
   And wait. 'Hullo . . .? Is anybody there . . .?'

Slowly, slowly, slowly the upturned glass begins
   To stutter across the wrinkled fake Formica:
'*Y-e-s m-y n-a-m-e i-s*
   Running deer – I am your spirit
guide . . .'

Then into top speed – our fingers straining
   To keep up – the glass careers across
The ruckled plastic (so fast, I can't believe
   That anyone was pushing . . .)

We had no fear. We had no sense of
   Dabbling in the darkest mysteries.
We didn't seek the keys to life and death:
   We wanted simple reassurance.

We had a formula; we always asked the same
  (Our litany of questions and responses) –
'Who will live longest? Who will be rich and
  Famous? Who will be THE FIRST?'

Each time we got the answers that we wanted:

Tim would be a rock star millionaire;
  I would be his drummer.
Rick: something scientific (never spelt too well).
  Pete would be a poet.

All of us would do great things.

So, for a few short weeks we kept it up –
  That long, hot, boring summer we were all fifteen.
Each day we'd go down to consult the spirits:
  Then come back and loaf around again.

And then one day we simply didn't bother:
  The phase had passed as quickly as it came.
We grew up – started GCE revision.
  The poet, rock stars, Nobel laureate became

A clerk, two English teachers and a golf club gardener.

Lads

I

Sitting in the boozer
    Saturday night,
    Dressed up right,
Waiting for a whisper:

'Heard of any parties?'
    Not a squeak.
    Things look bleak:
'Get another round in.'

Waiting at the bar when
    In they come,
    Dressed for fun –
This is looking likely!

Wait until they finish
    'Out the back –
    Come on, Jack!
We don't want to lose them!'

Lots of lights and laughter
    Pounding bass,
    'Here's the place.'
Put the party face on.

Walking through the door we
Give the chat,
Easy as that!
'Very nice to meet you –

Here's a can of lager – we were
Told by Ken.
You know, *Ken*
He said we're invited –'

Walking down the hallway
In the clear!
'Where's the beer?
Gonna be a *great* night!'

II

Standing round the table
Sloshing down the ale –
Brown ale, light ale,
Glug, glug, glug!
Danish lager, home-made beer
We're men, real men
So we drink beer!

Hanging round the table
'Let's have more!
See them? . . . Woaah! Bit of all right!

Let's have another,
Then we'll go and pull 'em . . .'
We're men, real men
Girls – it's your lucky night!

Blocking off the table
Elbows out:
'Spill my beer, John
I'll smash your face in!'
Ready for a bundle, ready for a fight
We're men, real men
So we get tight!

III

Last ones at the party – underneath the table.
'What's going on, Jack . . .?' (Who turned out
the lights?)

We drank what was left . . . in everybody's glasses
(Beer, Martini, barley wine and Snake Bites).

Must go home soon (. . . when the room's stopped
spinning . . .)
Must go home soon (. . . when I've sobered up . . .)

We had a laugh, then we were sick in the garden.
Men, real men (. . . till we threw up . . .)

Games

The rules were strict:

The First Eleven were allowed to call him
'Greg' – he liked that. The younger boys,
good at Games, could call him 'Mr Gates'.

But to the rest of us,
'the cripples',
he was 'Sir'.

The First Eleven thought he was terrific –
a real man, and a real good bloke.
I remember Greg Gates like a bad dream.

'Wot? No kit?' *Smack*
(a size twelve plimsoll).

'In the corner,
get that medicine ball

above your head
– *arms straight*!'

(We knew that teachers weren't allowed
to hit the pupils
in Maths or French – but this was Games;

we all knew that the school gym was
another country,
things happened differently there.)

'Oi, Johnson – what's your game?
Get in that shower!'

'But Sir, I've got a note –'
'You heard me, boy –'

'But Sir, I haven't got a towel –'
'Get in that shower!'

'But Sir, I haven't got a –' '*One* –'
'But Sir, I haven't –' '*Two* –'

'But Sir, I –' '*Three* –'
'But Sir –' 'All right, lads – throw him in!

You won't forget to shower next time.
Will you? Har! Har! Har!'

Full kit before, a shower after.
Undressing was a ritual.
We understood:

we changed for Games,
we left the normal world behind us
stuffed in a locker, hanging on a peg.

'Come on, Johnson,
don't be such a spastic . . .

everybody wants to try
the trampoline –'

On cue, the lads join in:
'Yeh, come on, Johnson –'

'Yeh, get a move on –'
Johnson tries a crippled rabbit hop

and gets the bird.
'Come on, Johnson, you big flid –'

'You woman –'
Greg Gates says nothing.

Then Johnson starts to bounce
a little higher.

‘That’s better. Now a front drop:
arms out, legs out – *go*!

Johnson’s chest hits
and his legs whip over.

(I’m standing at the far end
of the trampoline –

suddenly Johnson’s coming at me
like a rocket –

I duck, he hits the floor.)
‘*Gowar* – you great cripple,

why didn’t you catch him? *Damn!*
I think he’s bust his arm –

I hope you realize
it’s all *your* fault.’

And so it was, according to the rules:
we let him get away with it for years . . .
He’s still there now, as far as I’m aware.

‘You’ve got a *vest* on –
twenty press-ups.’

‘Wot? No plimsolls –’
Smack ‘– Have one of mine!’

Still got his medicine ball,
his corner: the same old games
and still the same old rules.

Innocence

It was the Hades of our school's mythology:
Behind the cycle sheds – the secret sinners' lair.
Deeds you could only whisper were committed there:
'Tracey'll show you *everything* for 50p!'

It was the Hades of our school's mythology

Ringed round with fag butts and the stale stink of pee,
Apprentice men puffed pilfered Woodbines, learnt to swear.
It was the Hades of our school's mythology:
Behind the cycle sheds – the secret sinners' lair.

Running in the Family

Is this the boy? Gawd, how he's grown!
   Be taller than his old man soon.
He's got his Uncle Charlie's hair
   So that's to be expected.

What does he do at school? . . . He plays
   The violin? I'm not surprised.
He's got his cousin Bertie's hands
   – Him what played the spoons.

I bet he draws and all . . . He does!
   Well, that's from Uncle Frank . . . You what?
Course you remember Uncle Frank
   – He done tattoos.

And Maths. I bet you he's a whiz
   At numbers – *Well*, with Grandad bein'
A bookie's runner all them years . . .
   You what? He's *not*!

Hopeless at Maths? You're pullin' my leg!
   It don't make sense to me at all.
Unless . . . *of course* – it must have come
   From *Her* side of the family.

Sunday Lunch

I

Cheryl! Dave's here.
Come on down and meet him –
She won't be a minute.
How was the drive – OK?
I'm glad.

Cheryl! It's Dave!
Hurry up, love –
She must be in the bathroom.
You did say you liked beef?
Oh, good!

Cheryl! Come on, love!
We're waiting –
She's really keen to meet you.
Getting all dolled up –
That's what it is!

Cheryl! Did you hear me?
Get a move on!
They take *so* long!
You know what
Teenage girls are like . . .

Cheryl! Come down!
Lunch is going to spoil!
        Yes – you go right on in.
        I won't be a minute –
        Promise!

CHERYL!
Come down – NOW!
        Oh, Dave – I'm sorry –
        Pour yourself a drink,
        Just help yourself.

CHERYL! (*OK! Then I'll*
Come on up and get you!)
        It's all right, Dave.
        You go ahead –
        Don't wait for me . . .

II

This house is mine and Mum's
  We manage fine, thanks.
We've never needed anybody else;

Me and Mum we get along *just dandy*,
  We share the cooking,
Cleaning, all the chores.

And we can change a plug or fuse,
  Don't worry. Hang
A roll of paper, paint a wall –

No need to fawn around some bloke:
  '*So* clever!' Just so his
Precious ego isn't bruised!

This house is mine and Mum's
  We manage fine, thanks.
We've never needed men around – *no way*!

We've got all we need
  We've got each other.
That's how it is – and how it's going to stay!

III

  'You must be Cheryl, how do you do . . . ?'
  'Your mother's told me *lots* about you . . .'
She could have warned me it would be this bad.
What am I doing here? I must be mad!

  'I often like to watch TV, don't you . . . ?'
  'I think your dress is nice, I really do . . .'
She could have warned me it would be this bad.
  'I think we're going to be *great* friends,
  don't you . . .?'

'Mum must have said – *I've* got a daughter too . . .'
'She's very keen on pop music, are you . . . ?'
What am I doing here? I must be mad!
'She's sometimes shy with strangers – just like you . . .'

Still staring at the ceiling – how's the view?
Your manners would, I'm sure, disgrace a zoo.
Most cows at least would deign to moo!

'You could have warned me it would be this bad –'
What am I doing here? I must be mad!

IV

How could she do a thing like this,
How could she?
Bringing a creep like him back home to eat.

Making herself look cheap for him,
Disgusting!
And after all the things she's said to me.

Who does she think she is? She's just
So selfish!
She never asked ME, never breathed a word.

All of a sudden – here he is
This Dave bloke!
Treating our house as if it was his own.

She doesn't see, but *I* know what
  He's after.
Smarming his crafty way into our home.

Holding her hand and dropping hints
  – Well, let him!
I'm going to see they're *never* left alone.

How can she bear to have him near –
  It's sickening!
He's such a slimy creep – why can't she see?

How could she fall in love with him?
  How could she?
How could she do a thing like this to *me*?

V

Just after Jack died
I felt like I'd died too.
I could hardly speak, see,
Think, move . . .

It's like living in a fog
That never lifts –

Like living underwater,
Floating, drifting –

Living in slow motion
Drunk on grief.

And always holding in the real hurt,

Keeping the real cries hidden
For her sake,
Until you're sure that
She can't hear, won't wake . . .

And then the hate begins.
'He's gone.
But I've been left behind,
Deserted –'

It's all so clear:
'If he had really loved me,
Would he have left me here
To cope alone?'

Layer after layer
To be stripped away;
Paring the feelings down
Until you reach the bone.

VI

In the end, it's loneliness that
Saps you, eats your soul away;
Like a small black rat –
Nibble, nibble, nibble . . .

The days have always been
OK. You get a timetable,
A system –
You run like clockwork

9 to 3.30: housework –
Washing, cleaning, ironing.
3.30: school's out –
Time to chat and smile and laugh.

But after she's in bed
The schedule's finished;
The nights are barren,
Empty, endless . . .

VII

– Dave?
He's not a second Jack, I know.
I'm not a fool – no matter what she thinks –
I'm not in love.

So how can I explain

How good it is to hear an *adult* voice,
To have to keep up with an *adult* mind –
And, yes! To have a man around again.

From the Japanese

The news: a film of
men watching a video
showing their future.

A robot factory,
the only human sound
the voice-over.

Obsolete humans
in perfect obedience
watch robots weld.

Dismembered limbs of
armoured Samurai
build automobiles.

'The Firm is certain
loyal workers will be proud.
You may applaud – now.'

An old man with a
little English, interviewed
for Human Interest.

The Company logo
printed on his baseball cap:
Quality Control.

'I see the future,'
he explains, 'and my
hands begin to cry . . .'

The Emperor's New Clothes

I

'The boy was late.
That's probably what started it.
He knew what time to be here
but there always has to be *one*
(as every teacher knows).

Bloody-minded,
insolent, hands in his pockets –
you'd have thought to see him
that a Royal Visit happened
every day. Typical!

So when all the
others marched into the playground
he didn't have a flag.
The only one – and served him right!
Yes, that's probably what

started it – sheer spite.'

II

The Family Therapist explains:
'These microphones are not
recording. Don't worry –'
he laughs, a little nervously.
'They're so my colleagues, there –'
he points to the mirror

'can hear you as well as see you.
So please, don't be nervous.
We're all here to help you.

Shall we start . . .'

The Therapist makes inquiries,
'Let's start with the recent
family history –' You what?

'New baby?' No. 'Bereavement?' No.
'Are Mum and Dad, well . . . ?' What?
'Well, *getting on*?'

The white and dial-less phone chirrups.
'Excuse me – *Yes . . . uh-huh . . .*
if you think so –' He smiles

embarrassed. 'It seems a good time
to take a short break –' and scuttles.
Silence.
Icy, awful silence.

III

Dad waits until they're in the car.
'You didn't say a word!
– Oi, you – *yes*, I'm talking

to *you*. We're doing this for you.
And what thanks do we get?
I hope you realize

all this costs money. And for what?
Bloody little troublemaker
that's all you are – isn't it?

Well?' The boy says nothing.

'Bringing shame on your Mum and me.
We're a laughing-stock now,
we can't hold our heads up.

Therapy? It's all a load of bollocks!
There's nothing wrong with you that a
damn good thrashing wouldn't put right.'

IV

'Well . . . up to a point he's making
progress. He's taking part
in all the normal things –

TV he likes and board games
with the other patients
of his age – but there's still

the underlying fixation.
Even under hypnosis he
resists, keeps insisting:

Look, look! The Emperor
is completely naked!
Those are his very words

repeated over and over.
I know it's worrying
for you, but on the whole

such extreme hallucinations
are a good sign. The worse
the symptoms might appear

the better our chances of a cure.
Try not to worry, your
boy couldn't get better

treatment anywhere in the world.
We're doing everything
we can, believe me – *everything*.

Prophet and Loss

The teacher says, 'I know
  By looking at their names –
Before I've even met them –
  Who will be a pain.'
He scans next autumn's register:
  'Emma, Tom and James
Will all work hard, do well.
  But Tracey, Shane and Wayne
Will be a nuisance from the start.
  It's plain,' the teacher says,
'I know by looking at their names.'

And by the year's end,
  He's been proved right once again:
'Work quietly, Emma.
  Less chattering, Tom and James.
Shut up, Tracey!
  You're in detention, Shane and Wayne!'

Passengers

I

When I was young and in the back seat of the car,
We played games to while away the journey

Like 'I spy with my little eye'. Or
My favourite: 'Alphabet pub names'.

Us kids would always be dead keen,
All straining to look out in front

'Look, *look*! The Zebra!
That one's mine – *I* saw it first –'

'Oh no, you didn't –' 'Yes, I *did* –
I've won! I've won! I've won! I've won!'

All Mum and Dad's idea (of course) –
Trying to teach us something all the time.

II

The same with Junior School – all *sneaky-learning*.
We never did a painting just for fun.

You always had to 'Name the colours – count the brushes'
'How many paint-pots can you fill from one big tub . . . ?'

But the best part was the stories, when the day was nearly over.
Heads down on the desks we heard

The names of gods and heroes, fearful monsters
Clang together: crack like bones in battle!

'Beowulf . . . The High King Agamemnon . . .
Odyseus . . . The Cyclops . . . Grendel's Mother!'

Names so good you *ached* to play the stories
Just to feel how good they were again.

III

But when the class moved on to New Street Comp
The games died.

First in the classroom: 'You're not here to *mess about* . . .'
Then in the playground, everything turned sour.

Teachers were trying to *Learn you* – force it in.
That didn't seem to work. That's when the shouting started:

'Shut up! . . . Siddown! . . . Belt up! . . . Pay attention! . . .'
Then even that stopped . . . in the bottom band.

We learned to keep quiet, not mess about too much –
Sit at the back, look out the window now and then . . .

IV

In this room, the teacher at the front writes
Slowly . . . slowly . . . slowly . . .

It's boring, but there isn't too much noise.
Another year and this will all be over.

From the back I watch the scenery that never moves.
We're passengers – just passengers, that's all.

Just passengers who haven't got a game
To stop the journey dragging on and on and on . . .

Leaving

I done a bonfire soon as I got home.
The last time! Yeah! Last day today!
I'm finished, never going back again!

I feel:
  Fantastic! Brilliant! Great! Terrific! *Magic!*

I piled the lot on – all the books and that.
History and English – useless waste of time.
None of it means nothing – not a bleedin' thing!

It felt:
  Fantastic! Brilliant! Great! Terrific! *Magic!*

Start work on Monday – *Cash!* – but even better
Nobody's gonna tell me what to do no more.
Nobody watching over, picking on me, nagging –

It's gonna be:
  Fantastic! Brilliant! Great! Terrific! *Magic!*

From *The Poet's Manual and Rhyming Dictionary*

Glorifying, magnifying
  Dignifying, petrifying –

Deifying, preachifying
  Churchifying, stupefying –

Prettifying, dandifying
  Frenchifying, putrifying –

Simplifying, specifying
  Classifying, mystifying –

Mythifying, prophesying
  Beautifying, falsifying –

Self-denying, qualifying
  Codifying, stultifying –

Verbifying, speechifying
  Trying, lying: *Versifying.*

All I really wanna dooo –
is baby be read by you . . .

A Level English – Summer 1999

Paper 1: Meaningful and relevant Scenarios

TIME: 3 HOURS

Candidates need only answer questions they can relate to in a meaningful and personal way.

Section 1: SHAKESPEARE

1. *Brutus*: Let us be sacrificers, but not Butchers . . .
   Let's carve him as a dish fit for the gods,
   Not hew him as a carcass fit for hounds.

Julius Caesar

You are the Roman undertaker in charge of Caesar's funeral arrangements.
From your professional point of view, do you think Brutus' plan (see above) was a success?
Demonstrate by drawing up a detailed bill for services rendered (in dinar). Be sure to show all labour charges (plus VAT at XIV%).

2. *Lady Macbeth*: Hie thee hither,
That I may pour my spirit in thine ear,
And chastise with the valour of my tongue
All that impedes thee from the golden round.

Macbeth

Imagine that Macbeth did *not* meet the witches on the heath (Act 1, scene 3) and therefore did *not* murder Duncan, Banquo, all Macduff's pretty babes, etc. From what you know of Lady M's abilities and interests, suggest at least THREE worthwhile and interesting part-time jobs for her now that she will not be Queen of Scotland and accomplice in the murder of Duncan, Banquo, all Macduff's pretty babes, etc.

Section 2: THE ROMANTICS

1. *The Sick Rose*

O Rose thou art sick.
The invisible worm,
That flies in the night
In the howling storm:

Has found out thy bed
Of crimson joy:
And his dark secret love
Does thy life destroy.

William Blake

If you were a member of the panel of *Gardeners' Question Time*, what advice would you give Mr Blake?
(NB Blake lived in central London; the soil is heavy clay.)

2. I fall upon the thorns of life, I bleed!

Shelley

You are the junior doctor in charge of a busy casualty ward in an east London hospital.
When Shelley arrives for treatment, do you:

(i) Give him a tetanus injection in the most painful way you can imagine and send him home?
(ii) Leave him to sit on a bench in the waiting-room for four-and-a-half hours to teach him a lesson for not looking where he was going?
(iii) Refuse to treat him until he agrees to take part in a series of clinical trials for a new laxative with unknown side-effects?

How would your behaviour change if you discovered he was a fully paid-up BUPA member?

The Last Ham

This is Papa–Oscar–Echo–Tango . . .
    Calling Yankee–Oscar–Uncle
This is Papa–Oscar–Echo–Tango . . .
    Calling Yankee–Oscar–Uncle

This is Papa–Oscar–Echo–Tango . . .
    Do you read me?
This is Papa–Oscar–Echo–Tango . . .
    Do you read me?

This is Papa–Oscar–Echo–Tango . . .
    Does anybody read me?
This is Papa–Oscar–Echo–Tango . . .
    Does anybody read . . . ?

This is Papa–Oscar–Echo–Tango . . .
    Is *anybody* there?
This is Papa–Oscar–Echo–Tango . . .
    Is anybody there *at all* . . . ?

This is Papa–Oscar–Echo–Tango –
    Mayday! . . . *Mayday*! . . . *Mayday*! . . .
    Mayday!
    Mayday! . . . *Mayday*! . . . *Mayday*! . . .
    Mayday!

. . – – – – – – – – – – – – – – ————————————